# CANVA

Professional Tips and Tricks When You Design with ~~ by Step Canva Guide for Work or Business with Pictures)

## By

## Patrick Ejeke

**This is My Way of Saying Thank You. You'll Also Get These Fast Action Bonuses...**

**Fast Action Bonus #1 – TikTok Marketing - Cheat Sheet** (Valued at $27)

This cheat sheet is a handy checklist that makes it easy to get started.

It breaks up the entire guide into easy-to-follow steps so that you can make sure you have all the highlights of everything covered inside right at your fingertips.

**Fast Action Bonus #2 – TikTok Marketing - Mind Map** (Valued at $17)

Some people learn better by looking at a mind map. The mind map gives you an overview of everything covered inside the guide. You can also print it out for quick reference anytime you need it!

**Fast Action Bonus #3 – TikTok Marketing - Resource Guide** (Valued at $17)

The Resource Guide gives you a quick point of reference to all of the resources mentioned throughout the guide.

This is my way of saying thank to you for buying this book. To get the bonus, **Scan the QR-Code below** to download the pdf and enjoy!

**https://www.easyimreviews.com/tiktok/**

the information herein, either directly or indirectly.

Respective authors own all copyrights
not held by the publisher.

The information herein is offered for informational
purposes solely and is universal as so. The presentation
of the information is without a contract or
any type of guarantee assurance.

The trademarks that are used are without any consent,
and the publication of the trademark is without
permission or backing by the trademark owner.
All trademarks and brands within this book are for
clarifying purposes only and are owned by the owners
themselves, not affiliated with this document.

# INTRODUCTION

In this book, I would like to present the step-by-step guide for Canva, a course that teaches you how to use it. After carefully analyzing the other courses and content about Canva on the platform, I took the time to think about 'How I could bring something different? How could do something that has not been made before with Canva?'

I try to put myself in my student's shoes and think about what they want when buying a book about Canva. Here is what I found out:

1. I would want to discover and learn how to use Canva.
2. I would want to be able to create the documents and visuals I need for my business.
3. I would want my instructors to be experts in what they are teaching.

So, I tried hard to make the best possible learning experience for you. I used a little bit of humor here and there to keep you awake. I use my book editing skills to make this whole thing look and sound as professional as possible. I just hope you like it.

Without further ado, this is what and how you will learn with me if you decide to buy this book.

In section one, I will explain 'why you need Canva,' 'why you should become better at design.'

I will make sure you feel comfortable using Canva and understand all the buttons and functionalities and assimilate the mechanics or fundamentals of using Canva.

Then my next target will be to teach you to *'Really'* use Canva. You will be learning about its cool tools and their way of use.

I will finish the book with a lecture that will help you decide whether or not you should upgrade to the paid version of Canva that is *'Canva Pro.'*

# THE SCOPE OF DESIGNING AND CANVA

The fact that you are here shows me that you are interested in design. Maybe you are in charge of designing important documents for your company such as annual reports, companies' brochures, or even project proposals. Or maybe you are the social media person in your company, and you constantly have to come up with cool photos, visuals, or infographics to populate your feeds.

Well, let me tell you one thing before we get started. Discovering Canva changed the way I work. I would not go as far as saying, 'it changed my life,' but it changed how I work.

Indeed, I do all these tasks I just mentioned for my company in Canva. I design documents, produce social media content regularly, and constantly create graphics to insert into my books.

I use Canva for 99% of these tasks; I barely use more complicated and expensive software like Photoshop or illustrator. So Canva not only has accelerated my workflow, but it has made designing more fun, more affordable, and quicker.

In Canva, you can use so many cool templates, and because I use Canva almost regularly, I have developed a better eye for design. As they say, when you are trying to learn a new language, the best way to do it is to surround yourself with native speakers. Well, I experienced the same with design by using Canva.

Constantly being exposed to good designs through templates, I have become much better at designing. It is quite amazing.

As you can see, I am passionate about this topic. I just love Canva. It has made such a big difference for me and my work that I am sharing this tool and its amazingness with you.

I have been working with entrepreneurs and small businesses for over seven years now, and I am horrified to see how much they lack a sense of a good design. No offense, It is not your fault. It is just the way it is.

So, I decided to do something about it and start my journey with this book to help entrepreneurs become better at visual marketing. I take this mission very seriously, and that is probably why I have spent over a month producing the best course possible about Canva and this for two reasons:

1. I am 100% convinced that in 2021, a good design will help you become a better entrepreneur.
2. I truly believe that Canva is the fastest and cheapest way to produce good design, even if you suck at design.

Not only many entrepreneurs and small businesses but also nonprofits and social businesses are struggling with design. But, unfortunately, many organizations often overlook design. But why is it so important? Well, just think about it this way; what is the first thing people will notice when they log onto your website or when you hand them your business card, or when they discover your Facebook page.

The first thing they will notice is *'the quality of your designs.'* Let me break it down for you: if your website, your business card, or your Facebook cover is ugly, your first-time visitor will keep that in mind as the first impression they make about your business.

Good design inspires trust. It makes your company look bigger than it is. Trust me, this is what you want for your business, and Canva will help you achieve just that whether or not you are good at design. Is not that wonderful!

# THE IMPORTANCE OF VISUALS
# IN TODAY'S WORLD

Every company has a story to tell, and as an entrepreneur, it is your responsibility to learn how to tell the story in the best possible way. Mastering the art of storytelling will open many doors for you in your company.

Today, visual storytelling has become a very important trend in digital marketing, and this for a good reason.

The average person remembers about 10% only of what they heard when tested three days later. Add visuals to your narrative, and that figure increases to 65%. So, visuals are great if you want people to remember your message. Visuals are also more effective than text at evoking emotions and inspiring your audience to take action. Both highly desired outcomes we are trying to achieve with marketing.

The Internet has completely transformed how we function in the world. There is so much content out there that people do not have time to consume it all. So the only way to get people to pay attention to your content is to be able to stop their eyes somehow.

Our age is characterized by an abundance if not an overload of information, and as a result, people's attention span becomes shorter and shorter. We have that tendency to jump from one piece of information to the next one very quickly because it is easily available and because it is free.

If you do not like one website, you close the tab and go to the next one. If you do not like this book, you just start looking for the next one. Well, you get the idea.

Let me tell you one fundamental thing I learn about marketing; *"to be successful in the market, you have to become a master at mak-*

*ing positive first impressions."*

In most cases, our visual perception of the world is what we use to form our opinions. Consumers discover and recognize companies through their brand's visual identity. They will start forming opinions before they even know who you are or what your company does.

Paying attention to it is very important. People will judge your ability to provide the solution they seek based on their first impression of your business, both online and offline.

So, do not risk turning away potential customers with an unprofessional brand. If your audience gets the wrong idea or is bored within the first few seconds of viewing an image representing your brand, chances are these people will just move on. Therefore, you should learn how to craft visuals that convey the right story. Invest heavily in the first image your audience will see.

In other words, learn to become better at visual design, and trust me, Canva will help you get there faster.

# USE OF CANVA

In this topic, I will teach you everything you should know to create designs with Canva.

**How to create a free account in Canva?**

If you are new to Canva, just go to www.canva.com. If you do not have an account yet, just go to the option where it says, *"New to Canva! Sign up."*

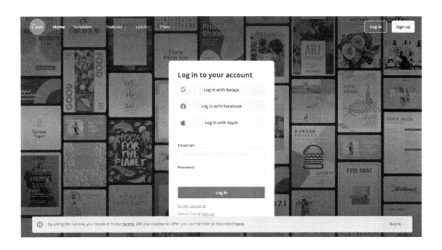

You can sign up with your Google account, Facebook, or your email.

When you log in with google/Facebook/email and enter your details, you will be redirected to the home page of Canva. First, I will explain how it looks, what are all the options, and then go to the design area. I will also give you an overview of how it is organized, what you can find in Canva. Then we will create a design, a static image for social media, and an animated video with moving elements with music.

## Introduction to HomePage in Canva:

As you can see, we have all these different options. They are categories, and you can browse through these carousels and check all the different categories that Canva gives us.

On the left area, you will see a menu. We are on the *'Home'* page but let us discover the other pages as well. Next up is *'All your designs.'* When you click, you will see all the different designs that you have been creating in Canva.

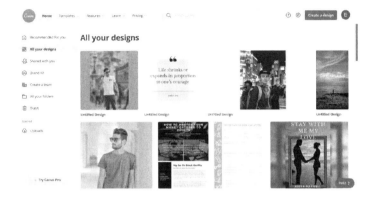

## Templates In Canva

After *Home*, the next option is *'Templates.'* There, we find all the different templates that Canva gives us for free, along with the premium ones. We can use all these templates and also customize everything that we see. There we can customize the colors, shapes, photos, fonts, everything.

If you are looking for something in particular, you can just type your keyword in the search box. It can be a social media such as Facebook social media platform, and you will see all the different options, or you can also type for something more specific.

For example, let us say, *'restaurants'* and you see that here Canva suggests 'restaurant flyers, gift certificates, logos, business cards, etc.'

They have so many different options and designs just for a single restaurant. So I will suggest you go there and check them out.

**Photo Library in Canva and How to Filter them**

Let us go to *'Photos'* that is the option that can be found in the *Features* after templates. They have a huge media library.

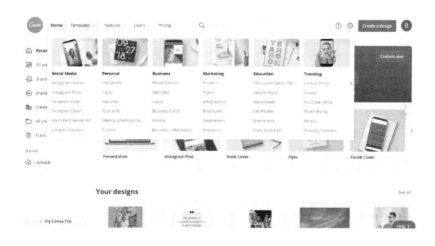

In the photo below, you can see we are in the photos library, and we can filter them by premium and free.

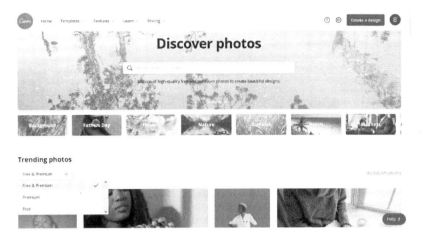

We can check all the free photos, use them in a design and download them.

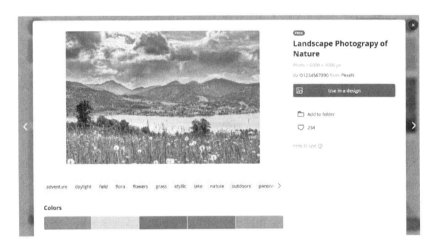

## Apps

We also have *'Apps'* as an option in the *Features* menu because Canva has all these different apps integrated.

We can use them for designing or for downloading or save images in other apps. So you can check them out. They have different apps and different platforms that we can use with Canva.

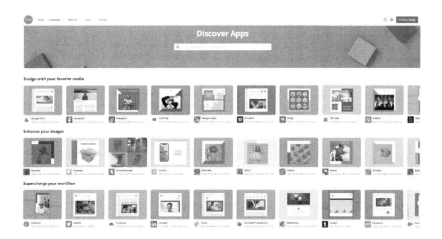

## Brand Kit

We have a **'Brand kit.'** This one is more interesting for pro users because, for the Canva free accounts, we cannot do much here.

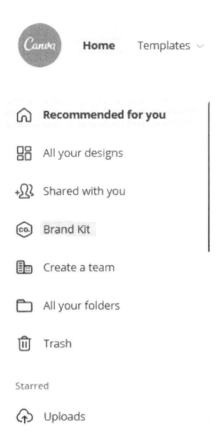

We cannot upload fonts. We cannot change these fonts here. We cannot add logos. We can just add three different colors to the color palettes, but that is all we can do. This brand kit is so amazing. I have a Canva pro account, and this one saves me so much time that I will recommend you checking it out.

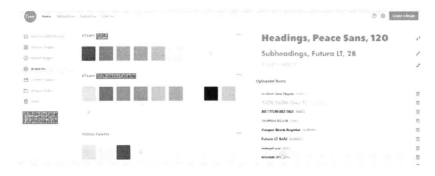

If you do not have Canva pro and you would like to try it for free. Canva will allow you to try Canva free for 30 days.

## Design school

There is the '**design school.**' So, Canva also has a couple of tutorials here which are free tutorials. You can just go and check it out. Everything is in English.

## Create a team

Then, we also have the '**Create a team**' option. I changed the team's name, but you can also change it for anything that you would like to name. For example, you can put here the name of your business or whatever you want to put here.

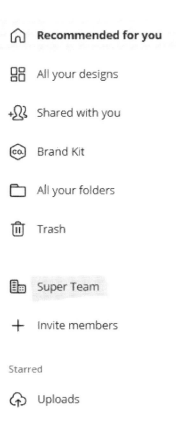

This one allows you to share designs with other people. We use that a lot, and it is very time-saving. It is really useful.

## All you folders

Then, we have the '**All you folders**' option. You can create many folders here.

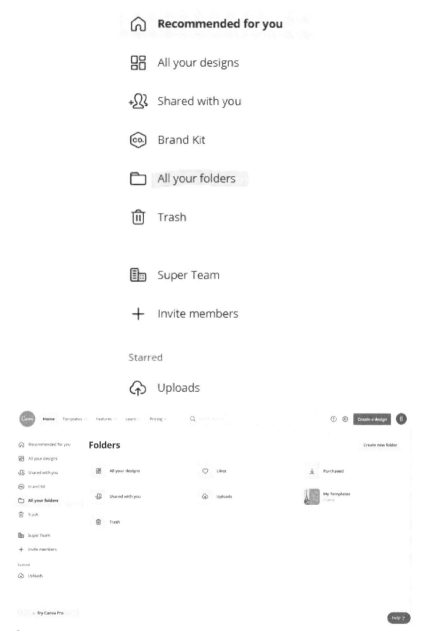

## Trash

And lastly, we have the **'trash'** area where you can save your designs the first 30 days when you deleted them; if not, they will be deleted permanently.

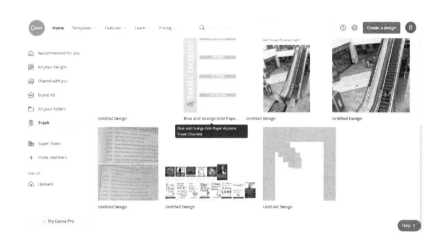

## Design Area

Now, let us start designing. First, I would design an animated video with some animated elements in the background and a photo with a nice filter.

Let us go to our Canva page, and for this, we will create an Instagram post. In my case, it appears here at the beginning, but if you cannot find it, type 'Instagram' and look for 'Instagram post.'

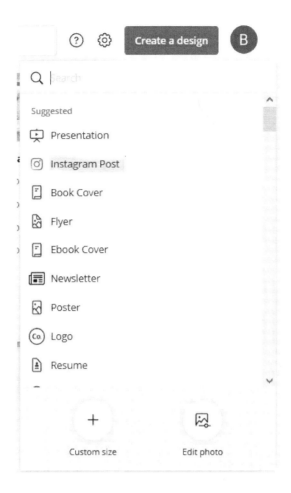

Canva will give you a bunch of different templates. You can use any of them. Here I will use a blank page.

## Design Tools and Their Functions

We are on this design page. Let us do an overview of this page. What do we find here?

- So, the first thing that we see on top is a menu, and we can find options like *Home, File, Resize,* and changing the name as I have named it as *"My Instagram post."*

- We have many different options, but the most important menu in Canva is the menu bar on the left-hand side.

At first, we have a bunch of different templates that Canva is suggesting for us or is suggesting. You can just go and see all here in this area. You can see they have all these designs organized by categories, and we can check them out.

- In this case, I will not use any of them, but if you want to use one of these, click on the design that looks interesting, and it will go automatically to your page.

- Next, we have '**photos**.' This is the same photo library that we saw initially. Again, it is the same – here, we have different categories, and then we can browse through all these photos or search for them.

- We have elements, and they also are organized by categories. So you see grids, shapes, frames, stickers, etc.

- Next, we have *'Text'* and *'Styles,'* where we have all these different text and color combinations that we can use in our designs.

Then we have the *'More'* we have all these different options for us.

- Here we have *'Audios,'* which is a really interesting kind of new feature in Canva.

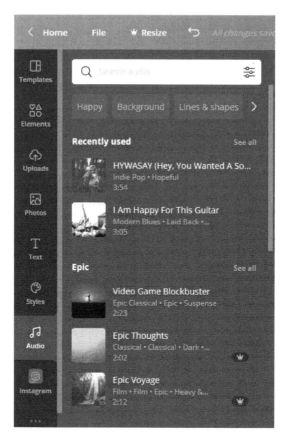

- *'Videos'* is also kind of new to Canva and really exciting. We can add these videos to our designs and give us a more engaging outcome.

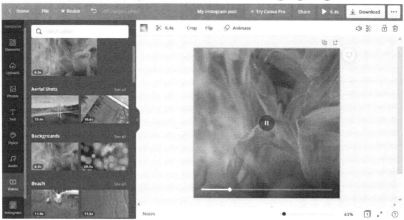

- Then we have **'Backgrounds.'** We can add textures to our backgrounds with just one click. We can also change the colors.

- You can change the color of the background. We keep the same texture, but we can customize the color.

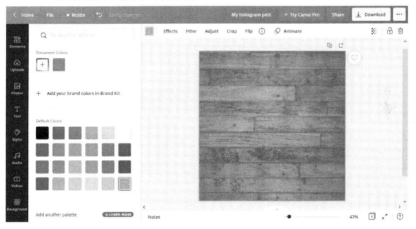

- We can also **_'Upload'_** our images and videos in Canva when we click the button upload and add an image or video. We can access our computer folders and upload our images or videos.

- Then, we have our folders where we can or-
ganize our designs. And save our data.

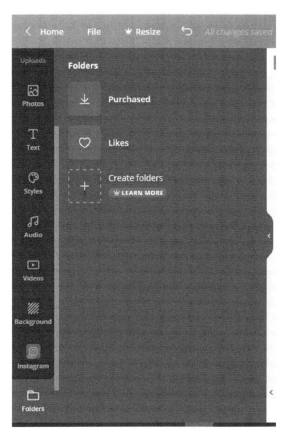

- Then in *More*, we have **'Apps and Integrations'** in Canva.

## How to create an animated post

Let us start from zero. So, the first thing is to open a design. In my case, it is an Instagram post. I have a blank page. Now I will add color to it. We can go background color and select one of these colors, or we can also open the color picker and select a color that we like. Then, we can change the things or add in a specific hex code of our color brands or any hex code that you would like to use.

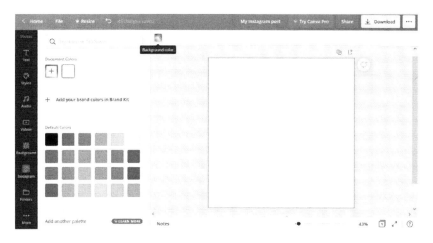

## How to use custom colors

In my case, I have my color here. So I am going to apply. So now, I have my branded color in my design.

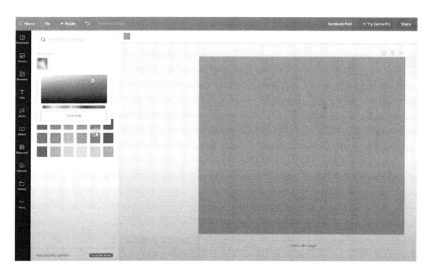

Next, I am going to upload one photo. I have already removed the background of this photo. This actually can be done in Canva pro; Canva for free does not have this feature. But there is this trick where you can remove your photo's background from the website

## remove.bg.

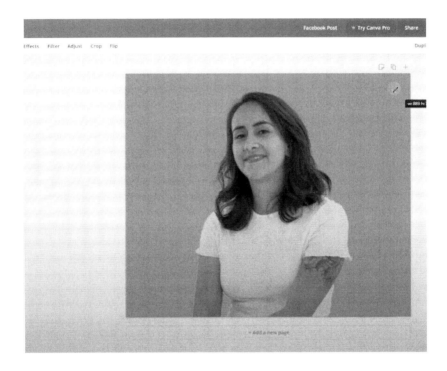

## How to remove the background from your photos

If you do not have Canva pro or you would not like to try it yet. You can use this website *"remove.bg."*

Let us go there, and you can upload your image here and remove the background automatically. If you use the free version, the images will be low resolution. So that is the only thing I do not like, but as I already said, you could try Canva Pro for free and use these remove background feature which is useful and exciting. I also want to add a text box. Let us add it.

Go to the text menu and add a heading. In this case, I want to create a post to welcome the new members of my group. So, I am just going to write here 'welcome.'

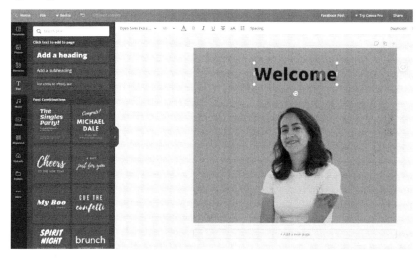

As you see here, when you click the background on this menu will see different options. When I click that text box, we will see some other options, different options for different elements.

For example, I click on the text, and I will see a menu for the text. If I click on the image, I will see a different menu to adjust the image. And, if we do it for the background, we will see some other options for the background.

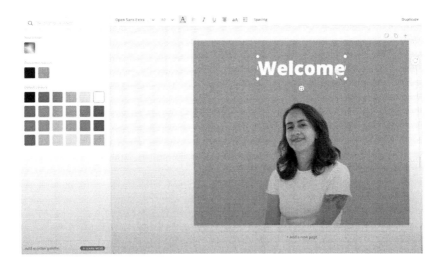

For the text, I will like to change the color of my text, and if I want to change the size, I will just click here and select a different size, or I can just do it with my keyword like this or with these anchors I can change the size.

## How to download video from Canva

If we want to download this image still as an image for Instagram or any social media, we can just click on the down arrow icon on the top right and download file type as PNG or jpg or even PDF, if you need a PDF.

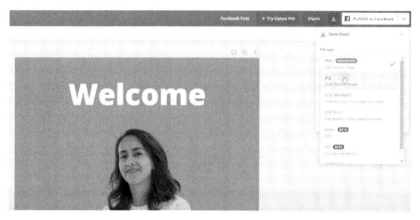

But in this case, as I told you, I want to show you how to create an animated video with some animated elements and music. So, let us do it.

Let us head to the *Elements,* and I told you that they have different categories so let us go down to the sticker category. Let us open it by clicking on 'see all,' and you can just browse through all these different categories or type something there.

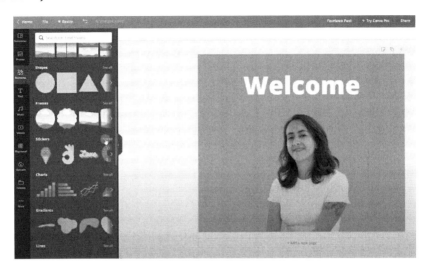

In this case, they already have the word stickers, and I will add another keyword. For this one, in particular, I will type blob and enter.

For this design, in particular, I will use these animated elements, and I will make it a little bit bigger with these points in the corners and points or anchors.

I am going to position this blob behind my photo and how do I do this. I will go there to this menu and click on the position and click backward.

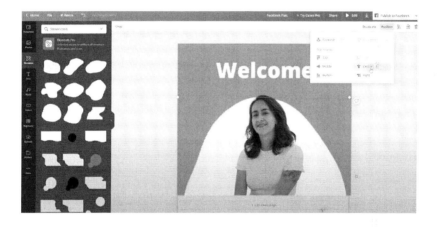

The element now is behind my forum, and I will position it to the center because it is not – I like the center. So click, and now it is a link to the center.

I am going to add another animated sticker or element. I will delete the word 'blob' in my search box, add 'brush,' and enter. I am going to select the first option of the brush here. It is an animated brush effect, and I will make it smaller and position it next to my welcome board.

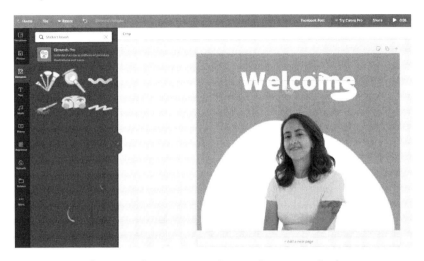

*So, here we have our animated post or design.*

The last final thing or the cherry on top will be music. Let us add the music. You can go to *More* and click on Audio. Go through all the different categories, and if you want to listen to one of these songs, just click on play on the top.

You can click like that and have a preview of the song. So, for example, if I want to use this song, I will click on the title and select the exact portion of this song that I want to use.

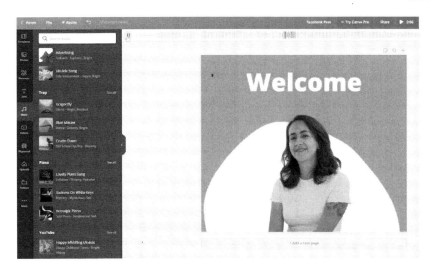

## How to apply a duotone effect on your photos

Click on the photo and then on *Effects*. So now, we have all our effects shown. To use the duotone, you will have to install it. Then, you just need to click on the duotone effect and connect.

Just select the effect, click and apply. We will have to wait just a couple of seconds until this effect is on top of the photo. So now, it is there.

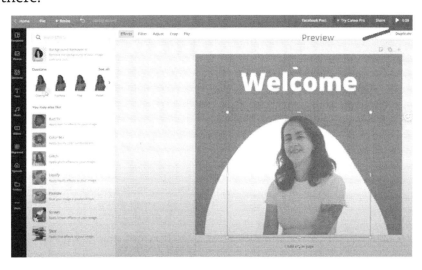

You can also preview the design here. Let us preview this. It is looking perfect.

*Now you can download it as a video.*

Now what I am going to do is to download this as a PNG. I want to show you this because, as we see, we have a moving element in the background and just wanted to show you that even if you use animated elements, you can also download these designs as PNG or JPEG static images.

# HIDDEN TOOLS IN CANVA

I will show you three free tools in Canva that you may not know yet on this topic. Since these tools are free, you can follow this tutorial if you have a Canva free account or a Canva pro account. So, enter your Canva account.

For the first tools that I want to show you, I will go to the templates section and select one of these designs.

For this exercise, I am going to select one that has a photo. So for this design, I would like to customize it a little bit. I would like to use another photo but give it a nice and cohesive color palette. But again, I know that creating my own color palette can take a while, and for all the colors to look nice and go really well together can also be difficult.

So, I will show you a trick, and I will say it is a hidden tool here in Canva that will help you in these situations.

## Photo Colors

First, let us change the photo. I have uploaded it here, and now it is time to change it.

Now that I have my photo here, I am going to select one of the elements. Select the background and go to the color menu.

As you can see, here we have different colors that say document colors, but also below this color palette, we see photo colors.

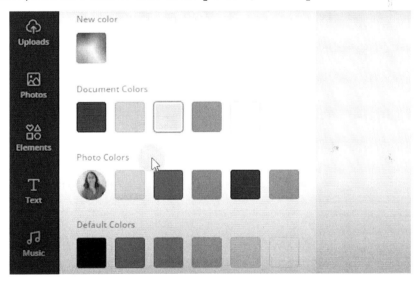

The photo colors are cohesive, a nice color palette that Canva created automatically out of our photos. This way, we can actually use some colors that will look really nice with the photo that we are using in this design.

I will select the background and use one of these colors, and then I will change the color of the other elements by using these other colors in this new color palette.

And like that, I can create a new design that is a little bit more customized, which goes well together.

I like this feature because I am making sure that all the colors will look nice together and complement the colors in the photo that we are using in the design.

I think this will save us a lot of time and help us with our design creation.

**Styles**

The second hidden tool that I want to show you will also help you create color palettes. Let us say that we will create a design like this one in which we do not have any photos.

So if we do not have a photo from which to extract or create a new color palette, where will we generate or take these new color ideas.

So, the hidden tool that I will show you today is here: you go to your left menu and go to *'More.'* Let us open this tab, and here you see this icon called *'Styles.'*

When you open it, you can see we have a bunch of different fonts and color combinations.

Let us go to the second tab, *'Colors.'* We have three different tabs *All, Color,* and *Fonts*. Let us go to the colors, and here we have a bunch of different combinations that we can use in our design.

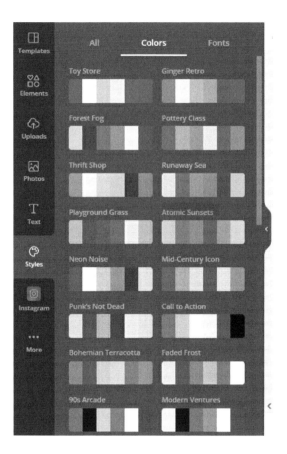

So, let us use the 'atomic sunsets' combination, and with just one click, I already have a different color combination in this design.

Let us try another one and see which looks better. We can keep clicking it to **Shuffle** all the different colors in all the elements and fonts and text boxes. And we can also keep clicking on the same color palette to get a different combination.

Let us see here what other combinations we can get with the same color palette. So I think this option is cool because we can get so many different color combinations with just one click. We do not need to go to all the different elements and try different color combinations. Canva is helping us here to get different color combinations. So yeah, we do not miss much time, and we can come up with more new and creative ideas.

We also have here the **Fonts** section and as I already showed you. So we have a combination of both. If we also want to customize this design, we can go to fonts and change the fonts.

Let us say that you are still not happy with these combinations. You can go here to *'All'* and try different combinations like font and colors simultaneously with just one click.

This cool idea is a cool functionality that will help us create new and more creative ideas.

I want to show you one more thing related to the styles tool if you have a Canva pro account.

Just remember this, we are here in the 'All' tab option, and we can only see already made or a pre-selected font combination and colors. But what happens if you have a Canva pro account?

Let us go to the templates and select just a random template for this example, and I am going to my styles functionality – let us open it. As you can see here, we have the options of brand kit.

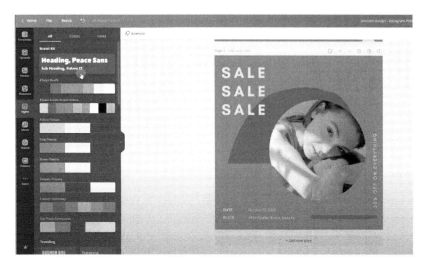

And if we go down below, we have the trending combination. Again, these are the same font combinations and colors that we saw previously in the free account. But with the pro account, we have our own pre-made font combinations and color combinations.

With just one click, I can have my fonts in this design, and with just one click, I can also have my branded colors into the design. Moreover, I can keep clicking on the color palette to try different color combinations.

But just to show you with the Canva pro account, you can have something even cooler because you can have branded designs with just a couple of clicks. And, you can change or create these color combinations and these font combinations.

If you go here to the 'home page' and then to 'Brand kit,' you can upload your fonts. You can upload them, and you can create several or as many color palettes as you want.

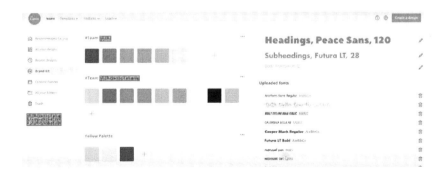

I find these functionalities especially amazing if you have a camera pro account. But if you have a Canva free account and still would like to try this feature, then I just show you the brand kit and to be able to customize your designs and make them look on brand.

## Rulers and Guides

The last hidden feature is quite new. For this, go *'File'* menu on the top left, let us open it, and click on *'show rulers'* and *'show guides.'*

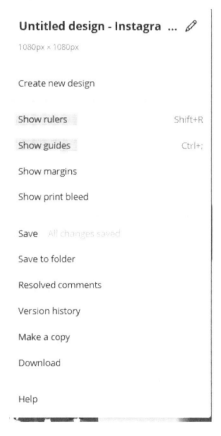

These two options were not available before. These are quite new, and let us click here on show guides.

After clicking here on show rulers, we have rulers on the top of the page if you did not notice. And on the side, if we want to create some guides on our design, we just click on the ruler and drag our mouse below or to the side.

Let us say that I want to create another page, and I want to position the text exactly in the same place as this page. So, to create a new page, click on *'add a new page,'* and if I want to add a new text, let us go for this one. I know where it should go with the guidelines because we created these guides on this page, and I can see them exactly in the same place or the same position on the next page.

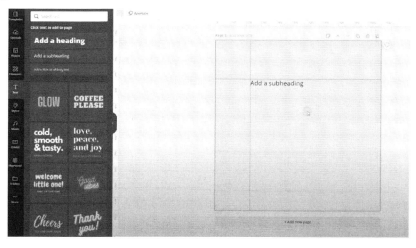

I think this is cool if you are creating designs with multiple pages, and you want them to look aligned and look organized.

# DUOTONE EFFECT IN CANVA

In this topic, I will show you three creative ways to use the duotone effect, how to use the duotone effect to change the color of your logos and create shadows. Also, we will create this effect in which we have photos with sections of different colors.

You can follow this guide if you have a Canva free account or a Canva pro account. Unfortunately, this functionality can only be accessed from the desktop at the moment. Still, hopefully, Canva will bring this feature soon to mobile devices too, but at the moment, we can only use it from our computers.

Let us go to the computer:

**How to change the color of your logo with Canva**

In this case, you see that the logo I have here has just one shade, and the background is transparent.

Maybe this color is not the best color that we can use in this design because the color in the background is dark red that does not suit the logo color. But, we can do better, and we can change the color of this logo to white. So, how do we do it? Well, we are going to use the duotone effect.

I have to select the logo that I have here. Then, we go to the effects button, and down here, you will see the duotone effect.

If you have not installed the duotone application so far, you can find it in the elements option when you scroll down.

Then you just have to click on connect, and you will have the duotone installed in your Canva in about five seconds.

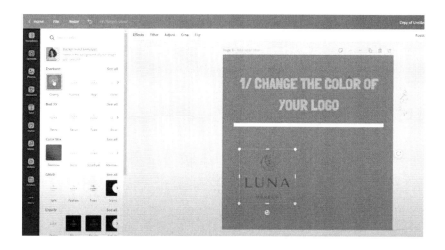

I am going to select the first one, and I am going to click two times. With the second click, I am going to change the high-lights and the shadows for white. In this case, I want this logo to look white, and then I hit apply. It is as simple as that.

Now I have my logo in white. I can also test different colors.

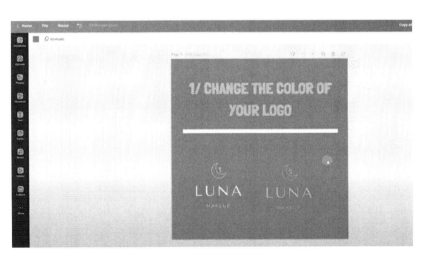

Let us do it. I am going to duplicate this logo, and I am going to do the same process again. Let us say that I want this logo to look yellow, and then I will use the same color for the shadows and then click on apply.

Just like this, you can have your logo in different colors.

# HOW TO CREATE SHADOWS WITH
# THE DUOTONE EFFECT

Here we have this design, and I have this crop-out photo. I am going to duplicate the image. Now, I have two times the same photo, and I am going to effects. I am going to do the same process we did before.

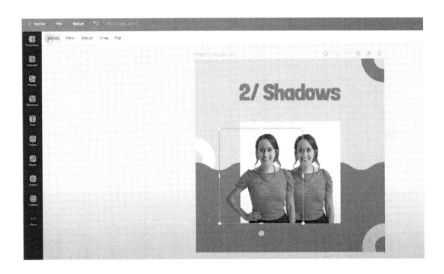

I can select any of the duotone effects. I am going to click twice and change the highlights and shadows to complete black and then apply.

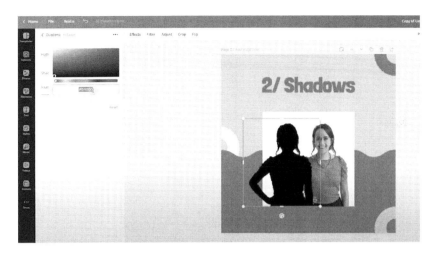

We will wait just for two seconds until this duotone effect is on this photo. Now, we go to the *Adjust* button. Let us go to the *Blur* slider and move it just a tiny bit to the right.

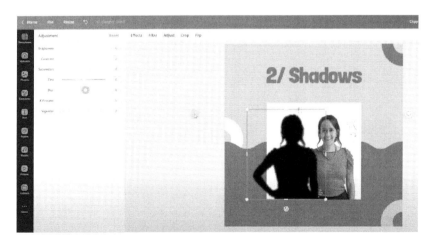

And now, I am going to position this blur or dark blur image behind the original photo.

Then I will reduce the Transparency, so the shadow is not so strong or not so dark that it looks natural.

## Creating different color sections in your photos

I will show you how you can use this kind of effect in your post on Instagram.

In Canva, I have a photo right here. I am going to duplicate it. I have two photos now. So, now, it is time to add duotone effects to one of the photos.

For this step, let us see all the different duotone effects that Canva offers. Now, the effect that I am about to use is the *Mustard* color. So, let us apply the mustard color to one of these photos.

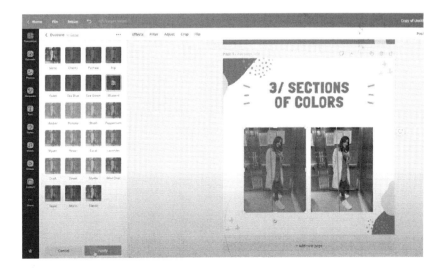

We are going to wait for just a second until the effect is on the photo.

Now, I am going to the second photo. Here I am about to use *Fuchsia* color for the other section of the photo. Apply, then just wait a couple of seconds. And now we are going to do the trick.

So now, we have the two photos. Unfortunately, the pink effect is only in a circle in the middle of the image. So, we will position the yellow photo behind and the pink or foxy color on top.

Now, recreate the effect we want; we need to crop the fuchsia color. So, let us go to elements and let us use one of the frames. I have chosen this rectangular one with two sides having ripped papers. It also has an interesting shape. I am going to position this frame here.

Now, I am going to take the Fuchsia color and bring it inside this frame.

If I go closer to the image, the effect is still not looking great. So I will double click on this frame, and then I will reposition the photo and then hit done.

*So like this, we have a different section of colors in the same image.*

## RIPPED PAPER EFFECT IN CANVA

In this tutorial, I will teach you how to create this creative and trendy effect, *'the ripped paper effect.'* You can use a Canva free or a Canva pro account for that. It is super easy and fast to achieve.

The ripped paper effects can be found in the **Elements** tab. Let us open it and let us search for 'ripped paper frames.' You can now see we have these new elements or new frames that Canva has uploaded.

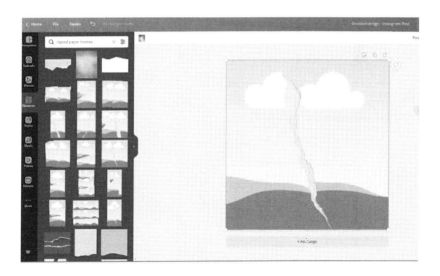

I would like to teach you two different designs because the frames have two different sizes, as you can see here. For example, this one has an Instagram story size, it is vertical, and if I use it on my square design, it will look kind of weird. So let us try to use one with a similar aspect ratio. For example, here, an Instagram post is the unsquared format, and I will use a frame with the same format, so it adapts and fits perfectly to my empty Canva.

The next step is to use you can use your photos or photos given by Canva.

So, let us say that you are going to use photos that are available here in Canva.

I want to show you to select the right photos and be very careful about how you position the photos. As you can see here, this photo selection goes better with this frame because we are not cutting any part of the body.

So, we will need to do some research and play around with all the elements and photos that we have here available in Canva and select the one that goes perfectly with the frame. And you are done.

## ADDING WHITE SILHOUETTE IN CANVA

I will teach you how to create a white silhouette or white stroke around your photos on this topic.

As you can see here, I already have a photo (Photo Without Background). I included or added this photo into a grid to not go to the background by accident.

I will duplicate this photo, and I will move it a little bit to the side so I can click on the background photo.

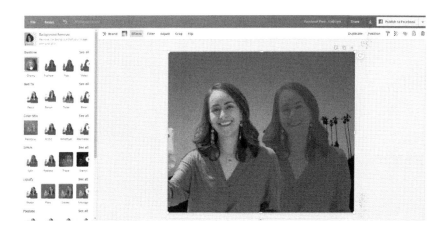

Now I am going to *Effects*, and I am going to use one of the duotone effects. It can be any of them; the color does not matter. Click on any one you like; I am going with the first one. When you double-click on it click, you go to the setting. Just like this:

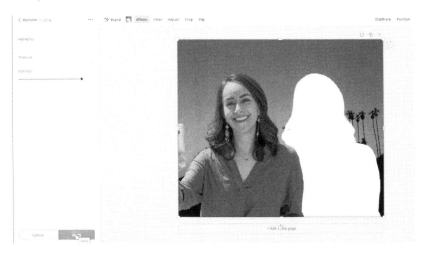

I am going to change the colors for the highlights and shadows to white color. Finally, click on *Apply* button and just wait a little bit until the effect goes to the photo or applies to the photo.

Now we are almost done. Click on the background photo and make it a little bit bigger. Then, I am going to position my photo on top of the white silhouette.

If you want to have a bigger white silhouette, you can also make it bigger and then align it to the silhouette with your photo on the front. It requires a little bit of patience. Just look around the photo, so almost all the strokes or silhouettes look kind of even.

## HEAD POPPING OUT OF A FRAME WITH CANVA

In this tutorial, I will show you how to create a head popping out of the bound effect, a photo cropped, but you can see that the head is popping out of the frame, and we will do the same thing in Canva.

I will show you two different styles, one with the round frame and the other one with a more creative shape.

You can follow this step-by-step guide if you have a Canva pro account that is the paid version of Canva. Although you still want to achieve this effect if you have a Canva free account, you will have to have your picture's background removed already. You can achieve this by going to *remove.bg* website.

**Out of the Bound Effect**

First, open your Canva account. For this trick, you can use either your own photos or use canvas stock library. I am going to use a photo that I have already uploaded to Canva.

The first step is to duplicate your photo. Now, I am going to use one of the features of Canva pro. I am going to select the photo and go to the *Effects* option. Then, I am going to remove the background with the option' *background remover'*.

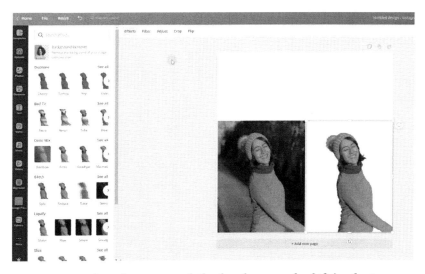

*Canva already removed the background of this photo.*

The next step is to go to *Elements* and select one of these frames. If you go down there, you will see the frame section. And click there on the *'See all'* option so that you can see all the different frames that Canva offers us.

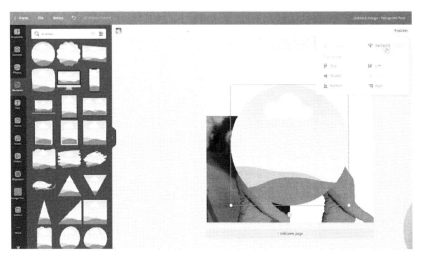

For this first example, I am going to use the round or circular one. I will make it a little bit bigger, position it in the center, and then change the position backward and backward.

Now, I am going to position the photo with the background inside the frame. As you can see in the photo, the head is still inside the frame. I need to adjust a tiny bit so my head is out of the frame, and if your photo is maybe too small or you cannot drag it upwards, so the head sticks out of the frame.

In the second step of this tutorial, the second trick I will show you how to take or make the head pop out of the frame.

**Avoid the photo getting cropped**

Now, I need to position the second picture (the one without the background) top of the frame. But if I position the photo on top of the frame, it is sucking the photo inside the frame.

So, what do we do for this not to happen? What I am going to do is to press Ctrl plus key and then drag the picture without the background on top of the frame.

And because I am pressing *ctrl,* the frame is not sucking the photo inside.

Now, I am going to match the photo (make it a little bigger). But, first, the two photos need to be perfectly aligned, one with the other.

**Make popping effect perfect**

To make this effect look nice, I need to add some transparency to the photo in front, which has no background. Now I need to pay attention to the details and position the photo in front of the other. As you can see, it is perfectly aligned now. It does not look displaced but perfect. You can, too, just nail it quick. Now, it is time to remove the Transparency. You need to bring it to 100 again.

As you can see, the hand and another part of the body are also popping out of the picture, which is not very aesthetic. So I just need to crop this part of the photo like this, and we have our effect.

**Creative Crop**

In the second part of this guide, we will create the same effect with a different shape. I will say a more creative shape.

Let us add a new page. For this example, I will use the photo library of Canva as they have a nice stock library.

If you want to use one of these photos or this exact same photo, you can type the name of the photo to find it, or you can also try to use some of these keywords together to find these kinds of photos.

I am going to duplicate this photo - remove the background. So now I have these photos without the background.

Let us go back to the elements, I already have here all the frames, and for this second example, I am going to use this frame ( the one that looks like a brushstroke. I like the shape, and I think it can add something creative to this effect.

Let us bring this photo inside the frame. And as I already mentioned, if you cannot bring your photo up to have the head out of the frame, let us just make it bigger, so the head is popping out, and let us crop it.

Now let us do the same effect or the same process as before. First, I am going to position the photo on top. Then, to be more precise, I will get closer and add some transparency to the photo on top.

It is really on top of the other one. Let us crop the part of the body that is popping out as it does not look very nice. Now, we are done.

# BLURRY BACKGROUND IN CANVA

In this topic, I want to show you how you can create a fake blur behind your portraits in Canva. This tutorial is for pro users only, so you will need a feature from the pro subscription, which is *'background remover.'* I just want you to be aware that this is only for paid users of canvas for pro subscribers.

I do not think there is a way you can do that without the pro subscription because you will need the background remover. The alternative would be to use the website **remove.bg** to get rid of the background of your photo and import that back into Canva. So, you can do that if you have a free account. Or, if you are a pro account, you can use background remover.

I will create an Instagram document, but again here, the document's style does not matter. We are going to go for a nice photo, a nice portrait of yourself with a background.

Let us go ahead and find one. Go to the *'uploads'* option to pick one of your photos with a background.

The first step is to position your photo on your canvas. Then the next thing I want to do is apply the *'remove background effect'* on this photo.

You need to duplicate the photo; that option is after the little plus *(+)* button.

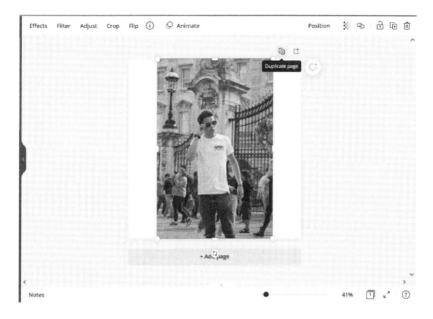

After duplicating the photo, you have the same photo right there; then, you will apply the effect.

Clicking on the photo - going to the effect, and then click *'background remover'* that is, if you are a pro subscriber. If you are a pro, this is how it will be shown:

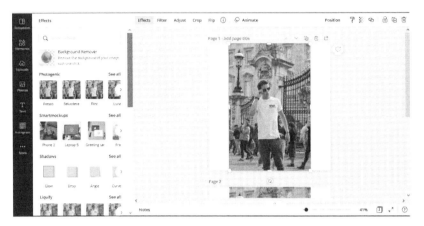

When you click on it, the background remover will do its thing and get rid of your background perfectly. It takes a couple of seconds because it is a hard job, and you have your background removed.

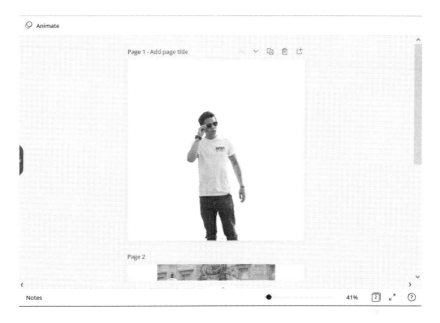

You will have yourself without the background there. But you still have yourself with the background on the other one that you duplicated before removing the background. So now, you can go back to the original photo you have with the background, click on the Adjust button, and use the *Blur* option.

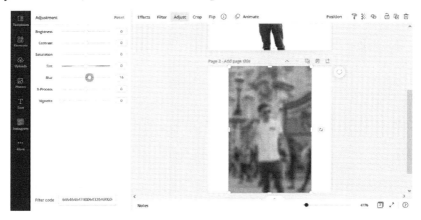

I need to click on adjust, and then I will add some blur to this photo – slightly blurring the photo is perfect, and now we are almost there. I just need to bring my photo back, and the trick is to simply position the photo (the one without background) exactly where it was, and you can now adjust the background.

You can get rid of the saturation. If you want to create some cool effects like black and white with only your photo sticking out, you could blur it more but then kind of loses a bit of its wow effect. You can play around with this.

The whole purpose of this tutorial was to show you how you can easily blur the background behind any portrait of yourself. So, the way to do that is to duplicate your photo, then remove the background on one of the photos, and then simply go back to the first one – blur the background, and reposition, and then you drag your photo without a background on to the photo that you just blurred. Then, you position them exactly so that you are at the same spot on both photos. But the background has been blurred on the base photo.

# INSTAGRAM CAROUSEL IN CANVA

In this topic, I want to show you how to create carousels for Instagram but not just any kind of carousel – we will learn how to create a seamless carousel panorama for Instagram. It is the kind of carousel that when you swipe to see the next image. It looks like the carousel is stitched together.

You can follow this guide if you have a Canva free account or a Canva pro account. I will also show you an app different from Canva that we need to create these carousels.

So, let us go to our Canva 'homepage', but before creating this design, I suggest you take a paper and a pencil and start taking note of all the content you want to share in this carousel. It will help you understand how many pages you need to create for this carousel.

**Using custom dimensions in Canva**

For this example, I will create a four-slide cursor, and to make everything easier, I will use a square format so because I already know that I want to have four pages, and every page needs to have the same size. I will use '1000 pixels per slide or per side', so the width will be (1000*4) 4,000, and the height will be 1000 pixels.

So, select *'Custom Size,'* add dimensions, and click on *'Create new design,'* and this will generate a very long format design.

Now, go to the *"Files"* tab and select *'show rulers'* and *'show guides.'* The guides are really important in this design because we need to understand where the slide is ending and where the other slide is.

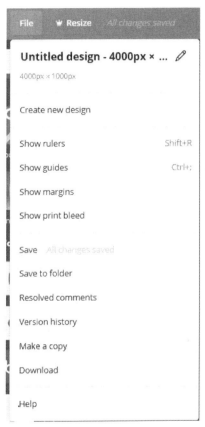

I will create one guide by just clicking and dragging my mouse. Now, because each slide will be 1000 by 1000, I will try to situate this guide into 1000. Sometimes, it is difficult to put it into the exact number of pixels, but we do not need to put it in the exact pixel. Next one I will situate 2000 and the other one in 3000.

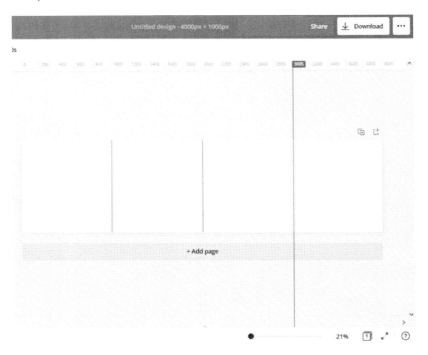

Now, it is easier for me to understand where to situate or position my elements and this design. As you imagine, I will create just one piece of the image, and then afterward, I will split it into four.

That is why I need lines to understand where the text is or where important information needs to be situated for it not to be cut in the middle and that people can read and understand all the messages you want to provide in each slide.

As you can see, we have our base ready; we are going to start designing.

So, I am going to start adding some elements to the page. The first element that I am going to search for is *'line'* in the ***Elements*** tab. I will need to scroll down until I find the exact element that I need.

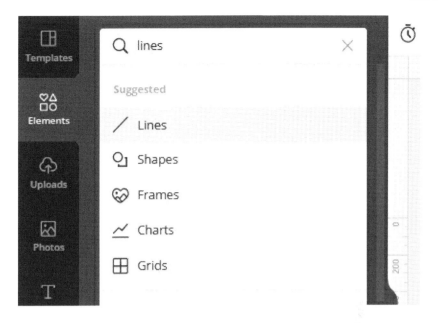

After searching a lot, the element I chose is the one u-shaped, or you can call it snake-shaped. I will make it big so that it is visible in the third and last slides. Then, I want to use this one and position it in a place where we can see it in the first and second slides. And then finally, let us add another one that will go in the first slide only. So, one has to play around it a bit to get that perfect position.

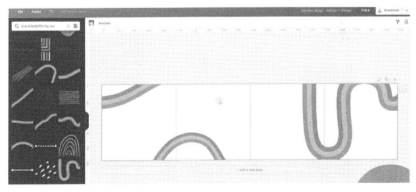

I am positioning these lines in very specific places because I want people to feel unity when scrolling in this character. So that is why

I am positioning these lines in these specific places.

Now, I will start adding some elements to make this carousel even cooler. I want this design to be very eye-catching. You can achieve that by adding the right colors. So, let us use some cool colors for the background – I will use purple here.

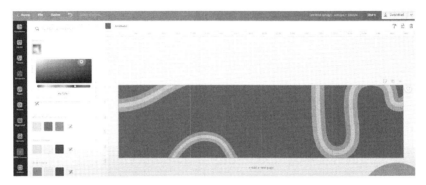

And finally, let us add some different colors to the lines. I will use a pink color and instead of orange. I will use another purple instead of sky sky-blue. Hence you can customize the line according to your color choice. I will apply this same style to the other lines.

Now, it is time to add two photos. I have already uploaded these photos into Canva. As you can see, the photos that I will use in this design have a white silhouette. I have already shown you how you can add a silhouette to the previous topic.

Let us continue with this carousel. Now, I am going to apply a *Filter* to these images. This one is called '*Streets*,' and I will copy the style onto this other image.

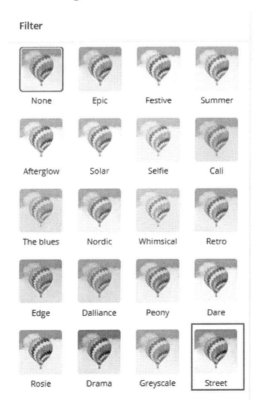

I like how these photos look with this black and white effect because it contrasts with the color in the background.

Now, we are just missing a couple of text boxes that we will position in each slide. So, I will do this quickly just to show you how it is done. I will use one font for the titles and another font for the text body or the little description that I will add to each slide. And, will also add a couple of images or icons that will make these slides or this carousel pop up.

The last thing that I want to show you is a website https://loremipsum.io, or you can google it 'lorem ipsum.' I will use this website right here because I want to use random text to describe these slides. I can position my description, but I do not have anything ready to write on these text boxes in this case. So I will use this lorem ipsum.

So now, I am going to teach you a little trick that I like to use sometimes, and it is to apply some text in the background to add a dimension to this design and something interesting.

I will just copy this title and paste the text right here. I will change the alignment to the left and also to the right. I will shrink this text box to see a part of the text on the second slide, on the third slide, and a little bit on the fourth slide.

And finally, I am going to position this text box to the 'backward' and add some of the Transparency just live I have shown in the image above.

The next step is to find an effect in which we have some texture into this design, but it is not interfering with the other elements in this design. So, I want people to read this text and see kind of something in the background.

We are going to add just one little element. You can leave your carousel just like this, but I want to use something that you can use only if you have a Canva pro account. So if you have it, you can use it; if you do not have a Canva pro account, just let it be like this, or use a free arrow.

So, let us head to the *Photos* tab, and I will type 'arrow paper.' It is an amazing element because it has a shadow, and it looks like real paper. It can add a different cool effect to this design.

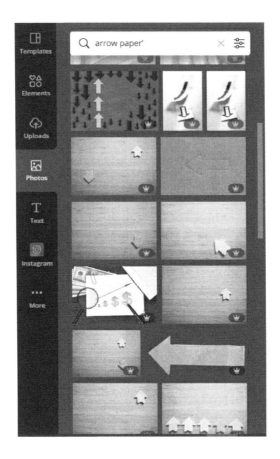

I will shrink it to see a part of this arrow in the second and third slides.

## Apps to cut the design

Now, it is time to teach you the app that we will use to cut this image for us to create our carousel into Instagram. So here we have this app called **'PanoramaCrop for Instagram.'**

This app will be available for android users. It is the one that I use, and it has been working well; that is why I am showing this up to you.

I know that many people are going to be asking, "Hey! But I have an iPhone. I cannot find this app in the apple store or Istore." I have this app for you. This one is called **'Unsquared for Instagram.'** I have not tried this app, but I know it is out there for iPhone users. It has 4.7 stars and 5,400 ratings.

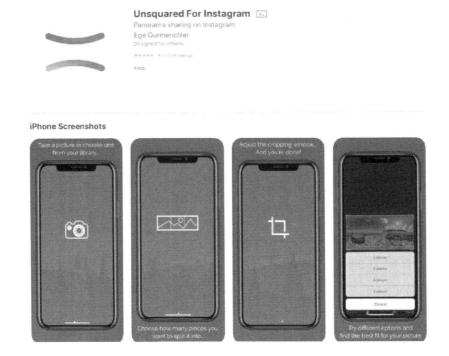

## How to download the carousel

So now, we have our carousel ready, we are going to download this as a png or a jpeg. In this case, I am going to download it as png. If you have a Canva pro account, I suggest you go 1.5 or 2 times the size because this will help your design have more definition.

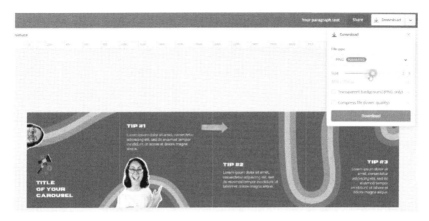

*Let us download this, and I will transfer this design or this image to my phone.*

Now, I am on the 'PanoramaCrop' app. We are going to select the first option that says 'New Swipeable Post.'

Let us click here, and now I will have access to the images I have on my phone. I have added my carousel, and the app is already suggesting cutting this image into four. It is perfect because I have four slides.

Let us click here on this 'check icon,' and you will view how your carousel will look.

If we swipe to the left, you will see that we have this seamless panorama effect on this carousel.

The final step is to click on the check icon, and you will have these images in the gallery.

**How to upload a carousel into Instagram**

Open your Instagram and click on this circle-like icon and select all four. It will allow you the ability to include more than one image in your post. In addition, it will allow you to create a cursor, so you select your four images or all the images you selected for this carousel.

 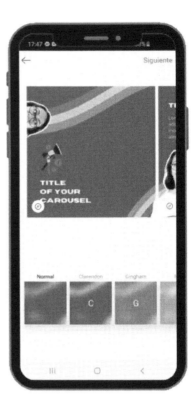

You will just click next and post your carousel to your Instagram. You can preview your carousel here before posting. If you want to change the order of your slides because you select the wrong order, you can just select one of the images and position it into the right order. Then, you are ready to publish this carousel.

## CANVA PRO VS CANVA FREE

Are you wondering if *Canva Pro* is for you? Are you trying to understand all the differences between the free and the pro version of Canva? If the answer is yes, then pay attention because we will cover all of this on this topic.

### Which features are included in Canva free?

When the founders of Canva decided to create Canva, the founders Melanie Perkins, Cliff Obrecht, and Cameron Adams have decided (I believe Melanie was pushing hard for this) that Canva needs to be a free product and remain a free product forever.

Canva is not only a free product but a free product that delivers a ton of value. That was the vision straight from the beginning from Melanie Perkins, and she is fighting hard to keep this a reality in the business.

Now let us cover all the goodness included in Canva, even if you use the free version. For example, IN the free version, you get the following:

1. You get access to drag and drop editor easily.

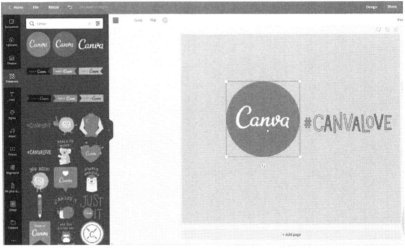

And that is what makes Canva so easy to use. You just drag elements from the left panel into the editor, and you start designing. You do not have to create from scratch.

2. You get access to video editing from the get-go with the free product.

That is a very interesting move knowing that many video editing software costs a lot of money.

3. You can use Canva on your computer but also your mobile, having that design on-the-go experience.

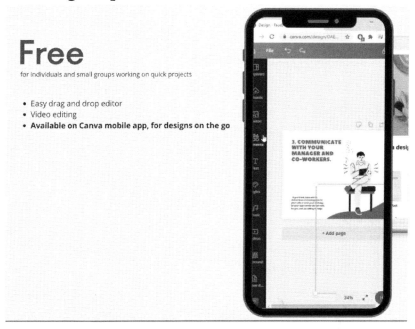

There are two ways of using Canva on your mobile. You can download the app on Android or iOS, or you can use Canva on a mobile browser – go to *canva.com* from your phone, and you can start using the browser version of Canva on your phone.

4. You can create a design with custom dimensions even in the free version.

From the Canva homepage, you can either decide to go with a preset, a document type that Canva is showing you; that could be a presentation, Instagram post, Facebook post, and YouTube banner, and so on – these are the presets, the document types. Or you can use the button ***Custom size*** and create a custom dimension project which is pretty cool, and they left this option open even for the non-paying users.

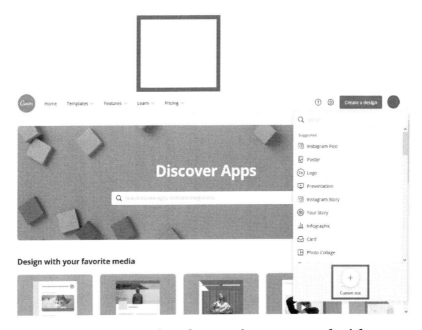

5. You can upload your images and videos.

You are not locked and just only limited to what is in the library. You can upload your photos, videos, and sounds, and even all of that is for free.

## 6. You have access to the text effects.

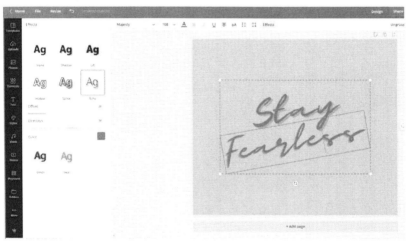

That is something that Canva could have easily decided to give to their paid users, as we have seen in many software. So, we have seven different beautiful text effects.

## 7. You can use the style tabs to shuffle the styles

of your design easily.

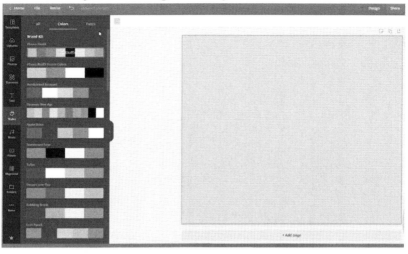

There you have some preset color palettes and font styles. Just by clicking on the styles tab, you can shuffle the way your design looks. It is like automating the visual designs.

8. You have a built-in social sharing and presentation mode.

In this presentation mode, you can easily design your presentations with just a few clicks and the same with built-in social sharing. You can create designs in Canva and share them on your favorite social media networks.

9. You have built-in commenting, which is a relatively new feature with the collaborative aspects of Canva.

You can now work simultaneously with more than one user in the same Canva document, and you can leave comments to the other people of your team or if you work with someone in another country, another city. So it is super convenient to now leave feedback within a Canva document. I love the commenting options.

## 10. Photo editing

You can import your photos, or you can use a photo from the Canva library. Canva gives you a different set of options to edit these photos like the contrast, luminosity, you can play with saturation, and you can use all of these.

You can have classic photo editing sliders and features directly from Canva. You can also play around with different filters that Canva has created for you. All of this is included in the base product in the free version.

## 11. Design and share with your entire team.

It is a pretty powerful option. You can create a design and make that design available to everyone in your team.

And, you can even share your designs created in Canva with people from outside your team who are not yet using Canva by just generating a link.

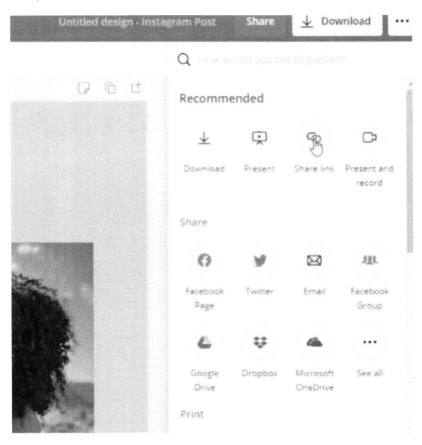

You will have an option to generate an edit or a view link for the free users and send that to somebody by sending a regular link. You can send that via email, you can send that via messaging platform, and invite people to collaborate with your Canva designs.

You can also share view and edit access to selected people in your team. If you do not wish everyone to have access to the same design, you can tick on and off the people, you want to share your design with.

## 12. Canva gave you many formats for your file.

Canva offers different exporting options, and even if you are using Canva for free, you can export your designs as pdf, jpeg, png, gifs, or mp4 for videos or even PowerPoints is pretty interesting.

## 13. You can publish designs to various social networks and apps

Canva is integrated nicely with Facebook, Instagram, Snapchat, and many other social media networks and even apps like Dropbox, Google Drive, or Flickr.

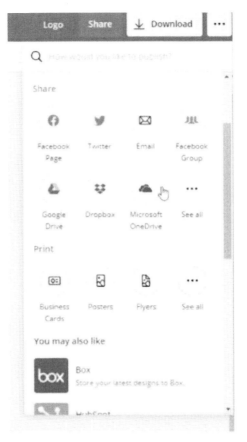

*You can publish directly to these social media networks or apps.*

## 14. You get access for free to all the Canva apps and integrations.

Canva is constantly looking for new partnerships and integration to make it easier for you to use it and publish anywhere.

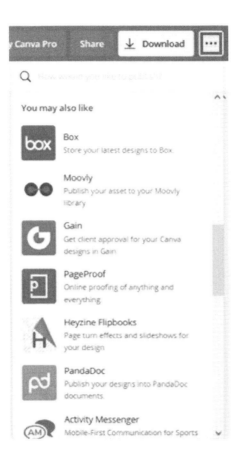

Look out for these apps under the three little dot menu, and you will see all the apps and integration.

You can almost do everything in Canva even if you are not paying a dime. These are the features that are guaranteed to be free and remain free forever.

## What is Canva Pro?

Canva pro is Canva's subscription product - subscription offer.

Meaning, it is a price that you will be paying monthly or on an annual basis, if you choose to do so, to get access to the pro features.

**Canva free vs. Canva pro features**

Well, here this little chart that compares in terms of numbers and features.

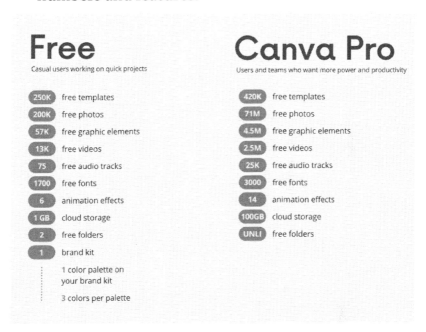

| Free | Canva Pro |
|------|-----------|
| Casual users working on quick projects | Users and teams who want more power and productivity |
| 250K free templates | 420K free templates |
| 200K free photos | 71M free photos |
| 57K free graphic elements | 4.5M free graphic elements |
| 13K free videos | 2.5M free videos |
| 75 free audio tracks | 25K free audio tracks |
| 1700 free fonts | 3000 free fonts |
| 6 animation effects | 14 animation effects |
| 1 GB cloud storage | 100GB cloud storage |
| 2 free folders | UNLI free folders |
| 1 brand kit | |
| 1 color palette on your brand kit | |
| 3 colors per palette | |

There are a couple of differences; the first difference is the volume of stuff you get for free.

Canva pro also offers a set of pro-only features.

## Pro Only Features

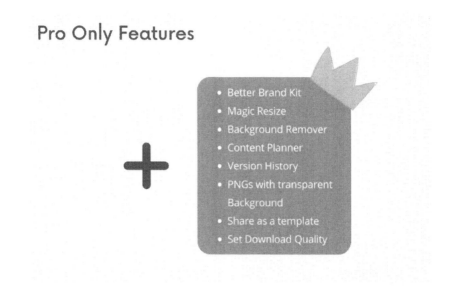

### Pricing

Let us talk about prices: How much is Canva pro?

If you go to *canva.com/pro,* you will land on a similar-looking landing page. It will be free forever for you, or if you decide to upgrade now that you know what Canva pro is all about, you can do it here from this landing page.

There are two prices. If you choose to pay for one year of Canva pro, you will be paying US$119.99. And, if you decide to pay per month, the price is going to be US$12.99. So, with a yearly payment, you save US$35.89. I recommend you go for the full year because then you save a couple of dollars every year.

**Is it worth upgrading?**

So, that is a big question. I have been using a pro for five or six years.

I know many people are using Canva, and they are very happy about the free version. So, I have prepared this little graphic for you that showcases what you are paying for when upgrading to Canva pro.

## Worth Upgrading?

- + 170K templates
- + 70.8M free photos
- + 4.4M free graphic elements
- + 2.48M free videos
- + 24.9K free audio tracks
- + 1700 premium fonts
- + 8 animation effects
- + 99GB cloud storage
- unlimited folders

- Better Brand Kit
- Magic Resize
- Background Remover
- Content Planner
- Version History
- PNGs with transparent Background
- Share as a template
- Set Download Quality

Again, upgrading it to pro is entirely up to you. If we come back to this question from the beginning of the topic, like 'is it worth paying for pro monthly for my business?' Well, it depends on whether or not you will need access to all of these media, photos, graphics, and videos.

Are you already paying for stock photos? When you need a photo, where do you find it? If the answer is *Yes*, then you can go ahead with a pro. You are already paying for stock photos and spending a lot of time going to some image library, finding the right photo and downloading, and then uploading into Canva.

Maybe it is worth paying for this amount of other free material that you get directly into Canva. It is more integrated. It is easier to find that might be something to consider.

Are you in need of some pro-only feature? Do you need to get rid of the background on some of your photos? Do you need to export in different qualities? Do you need to export without a background? Do you need to have access to a more elaborated brand kit? Do you work with clients, and they have their own brand identity that you'd love you could use in Canva? Do you need to upload your own font into Canva?

All of these questions should make up your mind about whether or not to upgrade to Canva pro.

## DID YOU ENJOY THIS BOOK?

I want to thank you for purchasing and reading this book. I really hope you got a lot out of it.

**Can I ask a quick favor though?**

If you enjoyed this book I would appreciate it if you could leave me a positive review on Amazon.

I love getting feedback from my customers and reviews on Amazon really does make a difference. I read all my reviews and would appreciate your thoughts.

Thanks so much.

P.S. You can click here to go directly to the book on Amazon and leave your review.

Printed in Great Britain
by Amazon

87194484R00075